Chinese Tale Series

中 国 神 话 故 事

Jingwei Filling up the Sea

精 卫 填 海

Adapted by Wang Yangguang

Translated by Liu Yonghou

Illustrated by Yu Jun and others

改编　王阳光

翻译　刘永厚

绘画　于　均　顾景一　王　鑫
　　　宋春燕　赵　勋　王志伟

DOLPHIN BOOKS
海 豚 出 版 社

First Edition 2005

ISBN 7-80138-533-0

© Dolphin Books, Beijing, 2005

Published by Dolphin Books
24 Baiwanzhuang Road, Beijing 100037,China

Printed in the People's Republic of China

The Great Emperor Yan had three daughters.

炎帝有三个女儿。

They were all beautiful and kind, and were the apple of their father's eye. They always played together when they were free.

她们都非常的美丽善良，都是炎帝的掌上明珠。她们经常在一起玩耍。

The eldest daughter was a skillful farmer. She could do all kinds of farm work.

大女儿是种庄稼的能手。耕耘播种，样样都做得很好。

3

The second daughter excelled in medicine, and could collect herbs in mountains and write prescriptions for patients.

二女儿精通医术，她能上山采药，配制药方，给人们医治百病。

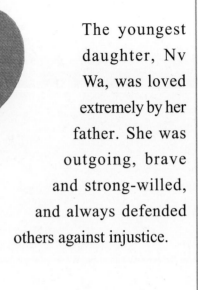

The youngest daughter, Nv Wa, was loved extremely by her father. She was outgoing, brave and strong-willed, and always defended others against injustice.

最小的女儿，名叫女娃，是炎帝最钟爱的女儿。女娃活泼开朗，坚强勇敢，喜欢打抱不平。

The Great Emperor Yan was always busy. He took care of the sun in the heaven and the crops and medicines in the human world.

炎帝平时非常忙，他不仅要管着太阳，还管着人间的五谷和药材。

The Great Emperor Yan had to go to the East Sea early in the morning to order the sun to rise. After a day's hard work, he arrived home very late after the sunset, overworked and exhausted.

炎帝每天一大早就要去东海，指挥太阳升起，忙碌整整一天，直到太阳西下才拖着疲惫的脚步回家。

Sometimes, Nv Wa had to stay
alone when all her family members
were busy.

炎帝不在家时，两个姐姐都要各自
忙自己的事情，女娃只好一个人玩。

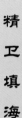

She wanted her father to take her to the East Sea where the sun rose, but her father was too busy to do that.

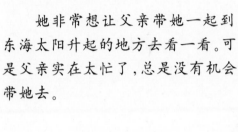

她非常想让父亲带她一起到东海太阳升起的地方去看一看。可是父亲实在太忙了,总是没有机会带她去。

One day, she went out to visit her friends.

这一天，她到外面去找小朋友玩。

The landscape was beautiful and Nv Wa was happy, though she felt lonely.

一路上，景色美丽。女娃虽然觉得孤单，但心情还是不错的。

Then she saw a big boy riding on a little boy.

这时，她看到不远处有一个大孩子把一个小孩子当马骑着。

The little boy looked very tired, but the big one did not get off from his back. Nv Wa got very angry and came over to them and said to the big boy, "Let the little boy go."

小孩子都累得要趴下了，大孩子还凶巴巴地不肯罢休。女娃走过去，指着大孩子的脑门说："你欺负小孩子算什么本事？放开他！"

The big boy saw Nv Wa was no more than a little girl, so he did not feel scared at all.

大孩子见女娃只是个小姑娘，根本不把她放在眼里。

He got off and walked up to Nv Wa, saying evilly, "I am the son of the Sea Dragon King. Who are you? Mind your own business!"

他从小孩背上跳下来。恶狠狠地走到女娃面前说："我是海龙王的儿子，你是什么人？竟敢来管我！"

Nv Wa said, "You are nobody at all! My father was the Great Emperor Yan, and I won't allow you to do anything bad here on land." The boy said, " I will give you a lesson. " Then he started to beat Nv Wa.

女娃不甘示弱，说："龙王的儿子有什么了不起，我是炎帝的女儿，以后你少到陆地上撒野。"龙王的儿子说："我先让你知道知道我的厉害，往后少管小爷的闲事。"说完，动手就打女娃。

Nv Wa was very brave and strong, for she often went hunting with her father as a little girl. She warded the boy's fist skillfully.

女娃从小跟着父亲上山打猎，手脚十分灵活，力气也不小。她见对方蛮横无礼，也不示弱，一闪身就躲开了对方的拳头。

And then she kicked the boy over. The boy didn't expect Nv Wa was so brave, and didn't know what to do.

接着，她飞起一脚，就将龙王的儿子踢倒在地上。龙王的儿子没有想到女娃这么厉害，一时不知道怎么办才好。

He stood up and tried to strike Nv Wa again,
but he was knocked flat.

龙王的儿子不肯服输，他站起来，挥
拳又打。可是又被女娲打了个仰面朝天。

Seeing that he was no rival to Nv Wa, the son of the Sea Dragon King had to give up and returned to ocean.

龙王的儿子见自已不是女娃的对手，只好灰溜溜地回大海去了。

Several days later, on a beautiful day, Nv Wa asked her father again to take her to the East Sea, but her father didn't agree and hurried away. So she decided to go to the sea on her own.

　　这事过去没有多久，一个风和日丽的早晨，女娃又嚷着父亲带她到东海太阳升起的地方去玩。炎帝还是没有答应，就急匆匆地走了。于是，女娃决定一个人去东海。

19

The colorful shells on the beach fascinated Nv Wa. She kept picking them while walking along the beach. She had already walked into the sea before she knew it.

女娃来到了大海边，被岸上五光十色的贝壳吸引住了。她专心致志地拣贝壳，不知不觉就走进了海水。

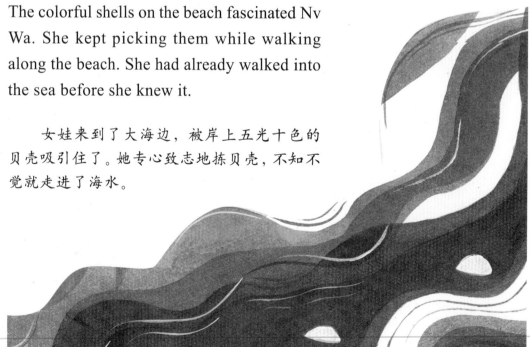

She enjoyed herself very much while swimming in the sea. When she saw the sea birds flying freely in the sky and the fish swimming leisurely in the sea, she felt very envious.

女娃在海中游泳，玩得十分开心。她看到天空中自由飞翔的海鸟和在水里快乐遨游的鱼儿，心里羡慕极了。

Suddenly, she saw a beautiful
palace not far away from her.

忽然，女娃看见不远处有
一座美丽的宫殿。

She got into a boat and rowed towards the palace. She rowed and rowed in the cozy breeze. The sun was setting, but she still had not reached the palace.

　　她坐上岸边的一只小船，就朝宫殿划去。海风习习，小船渐渐向大海深处划去。她划呀，划呀，一直到太阳落山了，还是没有划到宫殿前面。

It was getting dark. Nv Wa was very tired but she kept rowing. She was almost near the palace when the moon came out and stars were twinkling at her.

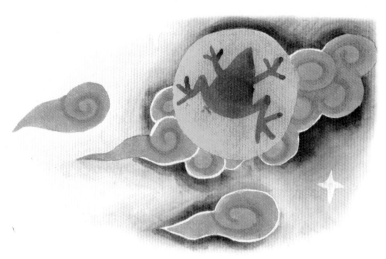

　　天渐渐黑了,女娃累坏了,可是为了到达宫殿,她还是坚持不懈地划着。月亮升起来了,满天的星星冲着女娃直眨眼睛。宫殿越来越近了。

Suddenly, the sea water was getting black and then began to surge.

就在这时，海水的颜色开始发暗。突然，海水沸腾起来。

The Sea Dragon King appeared and shouted to Nv Wa, " Who are you? Why do you come here at this time of night?" " I am the youngest daughter of the Great Emperor Yan. I am here just to have a look at the beautiful palace." Nv Wa replied.

原来是龙王来了，他非常生气地冲着女娃喊："你是谁？深更半夜的，跑到我家里来干什么？"女娃说："我是女娃，炎帝的小女儿，我只是想看看前面这座美丽的宫殿。"

The Sea Dragon
King said, "So it is
you who beat my son.
If you apologize to me, I will
let you go; otherwise, you will be
drowned." Nv Wa said unyieldingly, " It was not my fault."

龙王说："哦，
原来就是你欺负了
我的儿子啊，今天
你跑到我家门口，
赶快认个错，不然我
就淹死你。"女娲倔
强地说："我没错，认
什么错？"

The Sea Dragon King was annoyed and made the sea surge violently. With strong gales and big waves, the whole world became very dark. Even stars got frightened and closed their eyes.

龙王见女娃那么倔强，根本没有道歉的意思，立即搅动海水，掀起狂风恶浪。刹那间，天地一片黑暗，吓得星星都闭上了眼睛。

Nv Wa's small boat was tossed about like a leaf on the sea, and it was very likely to turn over soon, but she still continued to row calmly and bravely.

　　女娃的小船就像一片树叶，在海浪中飘摇，随时都可能被掀翻。女娃勇敢地面对恶浪，冷静地划着小船。

The sea was surging more violently. Nv Wa rowed the boat with all her strength and tried to hit the Sea Dragon King fearlessly.

龙王掀起了更大的风浪。女娲毫不畏惧，划着小船向龙王撞去。

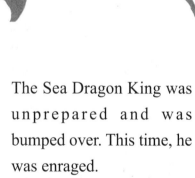

The Sea Dragon King was unprepared and was bumped over. This time, he was enraged.

龙王没有防备，竟被小船撞得翻了个身，他气得大发雷霆。

Soon, storms started to blow. It was lightning and thundering, and rows of waves as huge as small hills attacked Nv Wa. Nv Wa was getting weaker and weaker. She and her boat were at one moment tossed by the waves up to the sky, and the next thrown into the sea.

瞬间，海上狂风大作，电闪雷鸣，滔天巨浪向女娃涌来。女娃的体力渐渐不支，小船一会儿被巨浪掀到天上，一会儿又跌落在水里。

Suddenly, a huge wave swallowed Nv Wa mercilessly. She never came out again.

突然一个巨浪打来，女娃被大海吞没了，再也没有露出海面。

Day broke and the sun rose, but poor little Nv Wa died in the deep sea.

天亮了，太阳出来了。可怜的女娃就这样葬身在海底。

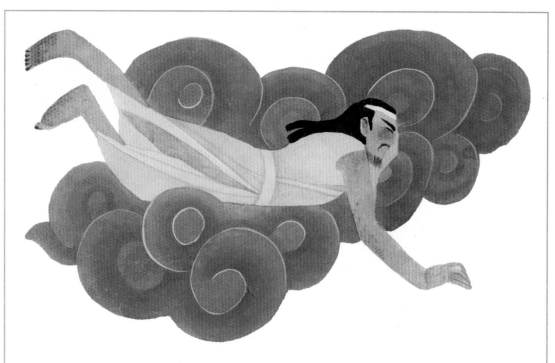

The following day, the Great Emperor Yan realized that his little daughter must have encountered misfortune. He came to the East Sea and was in deep sorrow. The sea was surging.
Where could he find his daughter?

第二天，炎帝知道女娃去了东海，一夜没有回来，就意识到了女儿一定遭到了不测。他独自来到东海边。只见大海波涛汹涌，哪里还有女儿的身影？

At this moment,
flying up in the
sky was a small,
color-headed,
white-beaked,
and red-clawed bird.

这时，天
空飞过来一
只小鸟，花
花的脑袋，
尖尖的白色
小嘴，小巧
的红色的脚爪。

The small bird was what Nv Wa turned into. As her sad tweets sounded like "Jingwei" "Jingwei", people called it Jingwei. Jingwei hated the ocean for taking her life away and was determined to take her revenge.

原来，女娲死后化作了一只小鸟，因为她总是发出"精卫、精卫"的悲鸣，所以，人们就叫她"精卫"鸟。精卫鸟痛恨无情的大海夺去了自己年轻的生命，她决定要报仇雪恨。

From then on, no matter whether it was sunny or stormy, Jingwei never stopped flying over the sea.

无论是赤日炎炎，还是狂风暴雨，精卫鸟一直在海上矫健地飞翔。

Every day, Jingwei carried small pebbles and twigs from the remote West Mountain to the East Sea.

每天，她从遥远的西山衔着一粒小石子，或一段小树枝飞到东海。

She threw the pebbles and twigs into the surging sea, intending to fill the sea up.

然后把石子或树枝投下大海，她要把大海填平。

The sea jeered at her, saying, "Small bird, you should give up! It is impossible for you to fill me up." Jingwei answered, "I will persist till the end of time, and you are to be filled up!"

大海嘲笑她说："小鸟儿，算了吧，你休想把大海填平。"精卫高声回答道："哪怕到了世界的末日，我也要把你填平！"

The sea said, "Why do you hate me so much?" "Because you killed me young and you will take away other innocent lives. So I will keep on working until I fill you up."Jingwei answered.

　　大海说："你为什么这么恨我呢？"精卫说："因为你夺去了我年轻的生命，你将来还会夺去许多年轻无辜的生命。我要一直干下去，直到把你填成平地。"

Then Jingwei flew toward the West Mountain again. She kept throwing twigs and pebbles into the sea for many years.

精卫又飞回西山去衔石子和树枝。就这样，成年累月，精卫往返飞翔，从不停息。

Seeing Jingwei was so worn out, the sun couldn't help feeling sorry for her and said, "Dear child, you should give it up! How can you fill the sea up with twigs and pebbles?" But Jingwei never changed her mind.

太阳看到精卫这样劳累，心疼起来。他说："孩子，算了吧，你衔来的树枝和石头怎么能够填平大海呢？"可是精卫一直都没有放弃。

Later, Jingwei got married to a salangane and gave birth to a number of little birds. The boys were all like their father, and the girls were all like their mother.

后来，精卫和海燕结成了夫妻。他们生出了许多小鸟。雌的像精卫，雄的像海燕。

The little Jingwei birds kept filling the sea just as their mother did. While the little salanganes fearlessly fought against storms just as bravely as their father.

小精卫们和她们的妈妈一样，也去衔石填海。小海燕们不畏狂风暴雨，搏击长空。

Up to now, Jingwei birds are still busy filling the sea. How brave and strong-willed they are!

直到今天，精卫鸟还在奔忙着，它们是多么勇敢和有毅力啊！

图书在版编目 （CIP）数据

精卫填海／王阳光改编；于均等绘；刘永厚译.
北京：海豚出版社，2005.10
（中国神话故事）
ISBN 7-80138-533-0

I. 精... II. ①王... ②于... ③刘... III. 图画故
事—中国—当代—英汉 IV. I287.8

中国版本图书馆CIP数据核字（2005）第115092号

中国神话故事

精卫填海

改编：王阳光
绘画：于 均 顾景一 王 鑫
      宋春燕 赵 勋 王志伟
翻译：刘永厚
社址：北京百万庄大街24号   邮编：100037
印刷：北京画中画印刷有限公司
开本：16开（787毫米×1092毫米）
文种：英汉   印张：3
版次：2005年10月第1版 2006年2月第2次印刷
标准书号：ISBN 7-80138-533-0
定价：15.00元